ARLINGTON

MAR 2 2 2005

What shall I grow?

Ray Gibson

Designed by Amanda Barlow

Edited by Fiona Watt

Illustrated by Kim Lane

Photographs by Howard Allman

Series Editor: Jenny Tyler

Contents

Green-haired creatures	2	Roots and shoots	18
A giant sunflower	4	Leafy stems	20
A tiny yard	6	Bean sprouts to eat	22
Sprout shapes	8	Tasty tomatoes	23
Tiny islands in the sea	10	A leaf into a plant	24
A spiky plant	11	Herbs on your windowsill	26
Crocuses in a silver pot	12	A sweet-smelling flower	28
Potatoes in a bucket	14	An ivy tower	30
Pots of pansies	16	A moss garden	32

With thanks to John Russell

Green-haired creatures

1. Wet an old sock and put it into a mug. Turn the top over the rim.

2. Use a spoon to spread lots of grass seeds all over the bottom.

3. Use an old spoon to fill the mug with potting soil.

4. Wrap a rubber band tightly around the sock. Chop off the top.

5. Pour water onto the top of the sock. Lift it up and let it drip.

6. Turn it upside down. Put it on a saucer and pour water around.

7. For a nose, carefully push a pin through one of the holes in a button.

To make a porcupine, squash the sock into a pointy shape.

  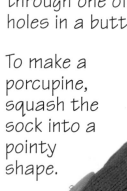 

8. For eyes, push in some more pins with buttons near the nose.

9. Put your creature into a warm, light room. Make sure you keep the top wet.

You can cut the 'hair' short and let it grow again.

You can grow these at any time. They take a few days. 3

A giant sunflower

1. You need to buy a packet of sunflower seeds. Put stones into the bottom of a small pot.

2. Fill the pot with potting soil. Press in two seeds. Leave a gap between them.

3. Water your pot. Put it outside in a light place. Water it often to stop it from drying out.

4. Two seedlings should grow. Pull out the smaller one so that the other one grows well.

5. When the plant is about as high as your hand, get help to plant it in a bigger pot.

6. Water your plant and leave in a light sunny spot, which is out of the wind.

Look on the seed packet to see how tall your flower might grow.

7. When your plant is as high as your knee, push a cane into the soil. Tie the stem on.

8. As the plant grows taller, carefully tie its stem to the cane higher up.

9. When the petals fall from the flower, leave the seeds on the plant to grow and ripen.

10. Shake out a few seeds from the head to plant next year. Leave the rest for the birds to eat.

Sunflowers have huge flowers and can grow very tall.

Plant your seeds in the spring.

Your plants will grow flowers in summer.

A tiny yard

Use small plants such as pansies, primula, ivy, trailing lobelia and alyssum.

1. Get someone to help you to make holes in the bottom of an old plastic dishpan.

2. Cover the bottom of the pan with small pebbles or pieces of broken pots.

3. Use a small spade to fill the pan almost to the top with potting soil.

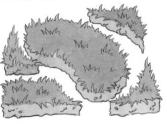

4. For a pond, make a hole in the soil. Put a shallow plastic carton into it.

5. Put small pebbles into the bottom of the carton. Fill it with water.

6. Cut a lawn from a piece of sod. Put it beside the pond and water it well.

7. Dig small holes and plant a mixture of small plants around your lawn and pond.

8. Put some plastic dolls' house furniture onto the lawn. Add a tiny cat or dog too.

Plant this at any time.

7

Sprout shapes

1. Tear off ten paper towels. Lay them on a large flat plate or a small plastic tray.

2. Use a spoon to put water on the paper towels. Add water until they are soaking.

3. Lay some cookie cutters on the towels with their sharp edges pointing down.

4. Use a teaspoon to sprinkle lots of alfalfa seeds into each shape. Do this carefully.

You can eat the alfalfa you have grown. Try it in an egg sandwich or a salad.

You can grow these at any time. They will grow in four to five days.

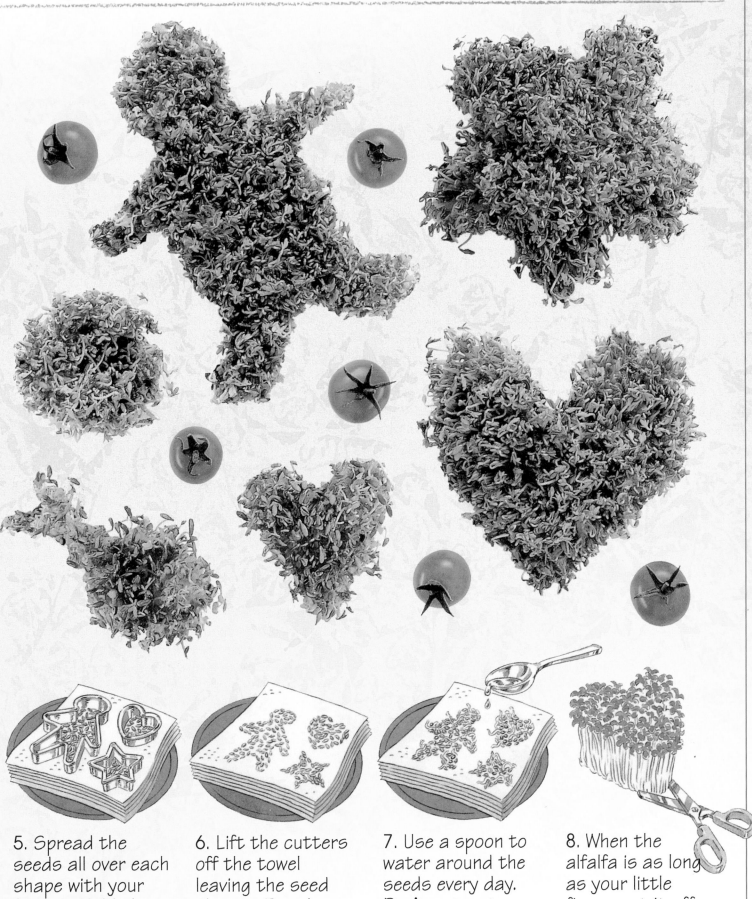

5. Spread the seeds all over each shape with your fingers. Hold the cutter as you do it.

6. Lift the cutters off the towel leaving the seed shapes. Put them in a light place.

7. Use a spoon to water around the seeds every day. Don't put water on the seeds.

8. When the alfalfa is as long as your little finger, cut it off so you can eat it.

Tiny islands in the sea

1. Cut the top off some vegetables which have sprouted a little. Cut them as thick as this.

2. Put a little cold water into a shallow dish. Spread the vegetable tops over the bottom.

3. Carefully pour in a little more water around the vegetable tops but don't cover them.

4. Put the dish on a windowsill. Add a little water each day. The shoots will grow in a few days.

Use vegetables such as carrots, parsnips, turnips and beets.

Your shoots should grow to look like tall trees on islands.

You can grow these at any time.

A spiky plant

1. Cut the top off a pineapple so that the yellow part of it is as thick as this.

2. Lay it on its side on a plate. Leave it on a windowsill for two days so that it dries out a little.

3. Fill a pot with potting soil. Put the pineapple top on top. Press more soil around.

4. Water it and leave it in a warm place. New leaves will grow in the middle.

Water your pineapple plant often.

Grow when you can buy a ripe pineapple.

Crocuses in a silver pot

1. Turn a pot upside down and lay some kitchen foil over it. Make a hole in the top of the foil.

2. Turn the pot over. Press the edges of the foil inside the top of the pot.

3. Use a spoon to put potting soil into the pot. Fill it about halfway up the pot.

4. Put some crocus corms (which look like bulbs) into the pot with their pointed ends up.

5. Fill the pot almost to the top with more soil. Water it so that it is damp.

6. Put the pot into a cool, dark place. Look at it once a week. Water it if it feels dry.

7. When the shoots are as long as your thumb put the pot into a light, cool place. Keep it damp.

8. When the shoots grow taller, put the pot in a light place. The flowers will come out.

Cut shapes from paper and glue them on the foil.

Plant in the fall to bloom in the spring. They take 10 to 12 weeks to grow.

When the flowers die, cut the heads off. Plant the corms in flower beds and they may flower again next year.

Stand your pot on a saucer to keep it from marking surfaces.

Try planting miniature daffodil bulbs in the same way.

13

Potatoes in a bucket

Eyes

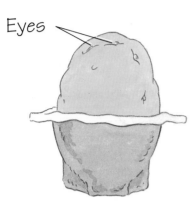

1. Put a potato into an egg carton, with its eyes at the top. Leave it for several weeks until it grows shoots.

2. When the shoots are as long as this, rub off most of the shoots but leave two which look strong.

3. Make holes in the bottom of an old bucket. Cover the bottom with stones then add some potting soil.

4. Push the potato into the soil with the shoots pointing up. Cover it with soil. Leave it outside.

5. In about four weeks, you'll see some shoots. Cover them with soil and water your bucket.

6. Add more soil and water it every time the shoots appear. Do this until the bucket is full.

7. After a while, flowers will grow. Water your plant often. If a potato appears, cover it with some soil.

8. After four months the plant will die. Tip the bucket over. See how many potatoes have grown.

Don't forget to water your plant if the soil feels dry.

Keep your potatoes in a cool, dark place until you are ready to cook and eat them.

Pots of pansies

1. Rinse the bottom part of an egg carton under a faucet. Let it drip.

2. Put some potting soil in the sections. Don't fill them to the top.

3. Put two pansy seeds into each section. Leave a gap between them.

4. Sprinkle some more soil on top of the seeds and press it down.

5. Cover the carton with a newspaper and leave it outside in a cool place.

6. Keep the seeds moist. After about two weeks, shoots will begin to show.

7. Take off the newspaper so that the shoots can get plenty of light.

16

For pansies which will flower in winter, plant in the late summer.

8. When they have grown two leaves, pull out the smaller shoot.

9. As your pansies grow, roots will grow through the sides of the carton.

10. Soak the carton and gently pull the sections apart.

11. Half-fill a pot with soil. Put one section into it. Add more soil.

12. Put your pots outside on warm days, but bring them in at night.

You can plant your pansies straight into a flower bed if you like.

Paint your pots with acrylic paint if you like.

Roots and shoots

1. Soak a big jar and peel off its labels. Soak three lima beans in a saucer.

2. Rinse the inside of the jar with cold water. Empty it out but don't dry it.

3. Fold a paper napkin in half. Curl it into a circle and slip it inside the jar.

4. Press the napkin against the side of the jar with the handle of a spoon.

5. Peel back part of the napkin. Push a lima bean in against the jar.

6. Add the other beans around the jar. Wet the napkin with lots of water.

7. Put the jar in a bright, warm place. Add water often to keep the napkin wet.

Leafy stems

1. You need a pot or a mug and some florist's foam (the kind used to arrange flowers in a vase).

2. Soak the foam in a bowl of water. Leave it in the water until bubbles stop coming to the surface.

3. Push the foam into your pot. Use scissors to trim it so that it is a little bit below the top of the pot.

4. Ask if you can cut pieces from plants which have woody stems. Make them just longer than your hand.

5. The pieces you have cut are called cuttings. Snip a straight end just below a leaf of each cutting.

6. Pull off the bottom leaves. Push the end of the stem into the foam near to the edge.

7. Arrange your cuttings around the edge. Push them in well so that they do not fall out.

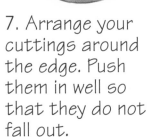

8. Put your pot on a windowsill but out of very bright sunshine. Water the foam often to keep it damp.

9. When new leaves grow, take the foam out of the pot and look and see if roots have grown.

10. Take a blunt knife and carefully cut the foam away from each cutting. Try not to damage their roots.

11. Plant each cutting in a pot full of potting soil. Water it and put it outside in a warm, light place.

Do this in the fall. They will grow in 6-8 weeks.

When you plant your cuttings, make sure that you don't forget to water them.

Cuttings in foam.

Rosemary

Box

Sage

Lavender

Ivy

You can plant more than one ivy cutting in a pot.

Bean sprouts to eat

1. Put two large spoons of mung beans into a strainer. Rinse them.

2. Soak the beans overnight in cold water. They will swell a little.

3. Lay some cotton on a plastic tray. Put water on it to make it damp.

Eat your mung beans in a crunchy salad.

4. Put two egg cups upside down onto the tray. Spread the beans all over.

5. Slide the tray into a plastic bag then put it in a black trash bag. Put it in a very warm, dark place.

6. Check each day that the cotton has not dried out. Water it to keep it damp.

7. When the shoots are this long, pull them off the cotton. Rinse them well.

    Grow them at any time of year. They take 4-6 days.

Tasty tomatoes

1. You will need to buy two or three small tomato plants. Get them from a garden center.

2. For each plant, put stones into a big plant pot. Cover them with potting soil.

3. Gently tip each plant out of its pot. Put one in each big pot. Try not to squash the leaves.

4. Add more soil to fill the pot. Gently press the soil around each plant with your fingers.

5. Water your plants well and leave them outside in a sunny place. Bring them in if it is frosty.

6. Water your plants every day, especially if it is hot and sunny. Flowers will grow.

7. As your plants grow taller, carefully push a cane into the pot and tie the stem to it.

8. After the flowers have died, little tomatoes will grow. Pick them when they turn red.

Plant them in spring and you'll get tomatoes in summer.

A leaf into a plant

1. Fill a small bottle with water. Don't fill it quite to the top so that you leave a small space.

2. Cut a paper square and fasten it over the top of the bottle with a rubber band.

3. Use scissors to cut off a leaf with its stalk from an African violet.

4. The leaf should be from near the outside and should look healthy.

Leave your plant in a light place, but not on a very sunny windowsill.

Grow at any time.

5. Hold the bottle. Make a hole in the middle of the paper with a very sharp pencil.

6. Push the stalk through the hole. Its end should go in the water. Add more water if you need to.

7. When tiny roots grow and new leaves appear it is ready to plant in a pot.

8. Make a hole in some soil. Put the plant in it and gently press around it. Water your plant.

Put your pot on a saucer. When you water it, put the water in the saucer, not on the plant.

Herbs on your windowsill

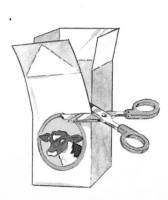

1. Buy some fresh herbs which are growing in a pot from a supermarket.

2. Wash out some empty half liter (one pint) milk cartons. You will need one for each herb.

3. Dry the cartons. Snip halfway down one side. Then cut the top off all the way around.

4. Turn each carton over. Make a hole in the bottom with the point of a sharp pencil.

Chives

5. Put some stones into the bottom of each carton. Spoon in a little potting soil.

Dill

6. Take each herb out of its pot by tipping it over and tapping the bottom of the pot.

 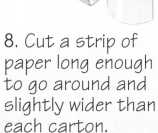  

7. Fill the gap between the carton and the roots with soil. Press the top of the soil.

8. Cut a strip of paper long enough to go around and slightly wider than each carton.

9. Wrap one of the pieces of paper around each carton. Tape it at the back.

10. Put your herbs onto a tray and leave them on a windowsill. Keep the soil moist.

Parsley

Basil

Thyme

A sweet-smelling flower

Grow a hyacinth in soil

1. Use an old spoon to put potting soil into a pot. Don't fill it to the top.

2. Gently press the bulb in the middle, with the bud on top. Add more soil.

3. Stand the pot on a saucer. Carefully water around the bulb.

4. Put it in a cool, dark place for eight to ten weeks. Keep the soil damp.

5. When it has grown as high as your index finger, put it in a light, cool place.

6. When it grows a little taller, put it in a warm place. A flower will grow.

Grow a hyacinth in water

1. Cut two foil circles and lay them over a tumbler. Press the bulb on top.

2. Carefully press the foil down all around the sides of the tumbler.

3. Lift off the bulb. Make a 2.5cm (1in) slit in the middle of the foil.

Rubber band

4. Snip the slit to make an X. Fill the tumbler with water, up to the foil.

5. Sit the bulb on top of the X. Leave it in a cool, dark place.

6. When the roots have grown long, move your bulb into a cool, light room.

Plant several bulbs together in a bowl, but don't let them touch.

This is a special glass you can buy for growing a hyacinth.

An ivy tower

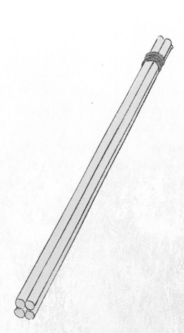

1. Put stones into a very large pot which has a hole in it. Fill the pot with potting soil.

2. Use a rubber band to fasten four short garden canes together near to one end, like this.

3. Spread out the canes. Push them well into the pot, with their ends nearly touching the sides.

4. Dig a small hole at the bottom of one of the canes. Put an ivy plant into the hole.

5. Add a little soil around the plant and press it down firmly with your knuckles.

6. Dig a hole at the bottom of the other three canes. Plant an ivy in each hole.

7. Hold the longest stem of each plant and twist it carefully around its cane. Water your plants.

8. As the ivy grows, twist each stem around its cane every two or three days.

Paint your pot with acrylic paint and put lots of Christmas decorations on your ivy tower.

A moss garden

1. Put a thin layer of potting soil into the bottom of a shallow tray, with no holes in the bottom of it.

2. Hunt for some moss on lawns, walls and between paving slabs. Look on stones and pieces of bark too.

3. Dig up small pieces of moss and put them on your tray. Add any mossy stones and pieces of bark.

4. Collect some rainwater if you can, but tap water will do, and spray the moss well every day.

Watch your mosses grow.

Add some shells too.

Grow at any time.